Swinging Doors

A Guide to Selling Your Company

by

Peterson Acquisitions

A Guide to Selling Your Company

Table of Contents

1

Introduction

Selling a business is one of the most important events in a business owner's career. This guide will help you understand each part of the process.

The masculine gender is used for the sake of simplicity, though we are thoroughly aware that there are thousands of successful businesswomen – buyers and sellers.

This is a quick reference guide for owners contemplating selling their business. In-depth financial and legal advice is beyond the scope of this guide. It is intended to give you a basic understanding of the process of selling your business and to help you avoid the most common mistakes. For more details contact a Peterson Acquisitions Consultant.

The best way to use this book is to read it before you begin to market your business and again throughout the process.

2

The Process
10 Major Steps Involved in Selling a Business

This chapter provides an overview of the steps involved in the sale of a business. Each step is covered in more detail in chapters ahead, but a general overview of the process will aid understanding.

Some steps may overlap. While each transaction will vary in its own unique shape and size, knowledge of the complete process will help get to a closing.

Step 1: Business owner decides to sell business

Deciding to sell is the first step. That may sound like common sense, but unless a business owner decides to sell, the process cannot begin. There are many reasons an owner may decide it's time to sell the business. Fatigue, retirement, or divorces are common reasons, but certainly not the only ones. Regardless of why a business owner comes to this decision, once a definitive decision has been made, the process begins.

Step 2: Determine the market value of a business

The ultimate value of a business will be the final price negotiated between you and the buyer.

Before placing a business on the market, a value or range of values must be established so that you have a basis for what and how to negotiate. There are many resources you can turn to in determining a business's market value such as your own knowledge, a CPA, an attorney, a valuation company, or business brokers.

A good broker may be able to help you price a business better than a CPA or attorney as a good broker knows the market and what things are selling for.

Step 3: Gather pertinent information into a marketing package

Unless the potential buyer is someone who knows your business intimately, such as an employee, customer, or supplier, they will need thorough documentation to understand the business. A business analysis must be performed to understand the strategic plan, financial statements, strengths, and opportunities. The resulting marketing package created is the first interaction a prospective buyer will have with a business; therefore, the old adage, "You can only make a first impression once" could not be more appropriate. The marketing package should include financials, and information about employees, assets, and the operation of the business.

Step 4: Market the business

Once you have gathered the necessary documentation into a concise and complete package, what's next? Potential buyers need to be approached and made aware of your business. When considering selling your business yourself, ask yourself if you would do your own dental work, re-wire your electricity or cut your own hair. You MIGHT be able to do it, but are you willing to take the chance you'll do it right? It's a tight rope over alligators that is better left to a professional broker you trust.

Step 5: Identify potential buyers

For every profitable business, there are prospective buyers in the market. The key is to establish who they are, if they have the adequate funding, and if they are a good fit.

A brief list of potential buyers includes: corporate executives, customers, suppliers, investment groups, and, on rare occasions, employees. It is crucial not only to identify the potential buyers, but also to ensure they are financially capable of purchasing your business. All potential buyers should sign a confidentiality agreement and provide financials to reflect an ability to complete the transaction. A number of pre-qualification methods can then be used to ensure a prospective buyer is financially secure, a good fit, and has a serious interest in your business.

Step 6: Meetings with both parties

The first meeting between a buyer and seller is similar to a first date. Each side wonders if the other likes them. The meetings with a seller are of high importance in a buyer's final decision. A buyer will rely on financial statements to determine if a business is being sold for the right price tag, but will often base the decision to buy on the relationship with the seller and the company's appearance.

Step 7: Offer to Purchase/Letter of Intent

After a buyer has met with the owner and completed the analysis of the financial statements, he will have three main options:

1. Pass on the business,
2. Ask for more details, or
3. Prepare a formal offer.

The two most common legal methods used for formal offers are a Letter of Intent and an Offer to Purchase. Both documents are similar; both represent an attempt to acquire a business. Most often, they are accompanied by an Escrow check, or Ernest money, which is a gesture of intent. This check is essentially a preliminary down payment on the total when the transaction is ultimately completed. If the transaction is not completed, the buyer will get his escrow monies back. However, if the buyer completes due diligence and has agreed to go forward in writing, the escrow check is usually non-refundable.

The main difference between the two documents is the level of commitment. A Letter of Intent is nothing more than a document stating intent of a buyer to buy a business. An Offer to Purchase is more detailed and outlines the commitment.

Step 8: Negotiate and structure the deal

Once an offer to purchase has been presented, there are three primary decisions: accept, decline, or negotiate. The sale price is only one of several negotiation points on an offer. Other variables are payment terms, length of training and terms for remaining employees staying with the business.

Step 9: Discovery

Due diligence on a business is similar to the second and third dates you have with someone. The beginning is mainly taking time to learn more about the other person, the business, and determines if both sides are compatible. Due diligence is performed by the buyer to ensure that the books, records, and operation of a business are as they have been portrayed. If it is a well-running company, then the due diligence should be effortless. If there are problems with the business, then due diligence may take longer and be more complicated.

Step10: Closing

Once you and your buyer negotiate the fine points of a deal, it's time to schedule the sale closing. The closing will follow the instructions provided when the escrow account was established. The escrow officer will confirm that all obligations and contingencies listed in the letter of intent to purchase and in the escrow instructions have been addressed. You and the buyer will sign closing documents. The escrow agent will transfer funds and record the sale and the agreed-upon transition to the new owner will begin.

3

Timing is Everything
Deciding When to Sell

A business owner can spend his entire career developing a business. It's his "baby." Selling can be the most difficult decision a business owner will make. It is filled with emotions similar to sending a child off to college or giving a daughter away at her wedding. The timing and reasoning for selling must be right.

The reason for selling will also be a paramount issue for a prospective buyer. A buyer needs to be assured that the reason for selling is not due to negative factors such as problems in the industry, increased competition, or employee problems.

Many owners tell us they are waiting for the best time to sell. The problem is that no one can ever predict when that time will be unless they have a crystal ball and can predict the future. Fortunately, the best time to sell can be determined by the common set of factors listed below.

Shelf life

If you have lost your passion for the business, hate going to the office, and cannot wait to leave, then it's time. Burnout and boredom are the most common reasons for an owner to sell his business. If cash flow has bottomed out for a few years it may be a sign of an owner who could work harder to drive the business forward but has lost the desire to do so. If cash flows have cratered or started to decline, it's time to suck it up and sell before it's too late.

If you experience burnout, one of the worst things you can do is hold on and let cash flow gradually decline, year by year. When or if you do decide to sell, declining cash flow will have a negative effect on sale price. A good buyer will see that an additional capital injection and significant effort will have to be executed before this situation can be fixed. The main lesson in this scenario is that the best time to sell is when an owner is able to detect his shelf life and get out when he can.

Retirement (age)

Want to work until you are 80? Do you want to wait until 65? What if 65 or 80 don't come around for you? If you could retire at 40 would you? Too often we talk to people who have a dead set age in their mind of when they want to retire. There is no time like the present to go live instead of work, no matter what walk of life you trek.

Health

 A sale is sometimes necessary due to the health of the owner. Structuring a deal for a quick sale due to the owner's health does not have to be for a lower price. A seller can set up a low down payment and an owner financing note for a longer period of time which will keep the sale price at the highest justifiable level, while getting the owner out quickly.

Market Factors

In addition to being ready to sell and having a solid profitable business, the economic marketplace must have its "stars" aligned in order for it to be a good time to sell.

A business doesn't run in a vacuum. External forces not only affect the growth of a business, but also its marketability. An ideal scenario to sell is when there is a strong economic environment of low interest rates, a growing stock market, a strong dollar, low inflation, low taxes, and a solid availability of capital. It is always a good idea to keep up with economic trends. While a bad economic setting does not help a sale, a good, profitable business will sell in good or bad economic conditions.

Shorter Stick Loses the Fight

If it were not for capital concerns, many business owners might never sell. There comes a point when the continued worry of funding accounts receivable, payroll or the rent will push a business owner over the edge. A business can actually become harder to handle financially with increased cash flow, even though there is more money generated by the business.

There is also the dilemma of growing a business to its maximum point and not being able to go beyond due to a lack of funding or managerial ability. You say to yourself, "If I just had some more capital I could do X, Y and Z and double the business." We've represented many owners who have reached a comfort level in their operations and do not want or feel comfortable with investing more capital to get the business to the next level. This is similar to burnout. A business will flatten out due to a lack of owner motivation. The salability will suffer and the sale price will be reduced if the owner stays put in this condition.

Industry overview

To know the future of an industry, it helps if you have a genie in a bottle to tell you the answers. If the industry is heading in a bad direction, it is time to evaluate the options though it would be unwise to suggest that every time an industry dips or change occurs an owner should think about selling.

But it's amazing how rare it is for successful business owners to keep up with their own industry. A common response is "I can't do anything about it, so why worry?" The more aware an owner is of upcoming changes in his industry, the more prepared he will be to look at his options. The most successful sellers we have represented were usually the best informed regarding their industry and economic setting. Informed sellers regularly attend local industry conventions and read trade publications, etc. These owners can talk on an informed basis about both economic and industry trends and make it procedural to understand quarterly changes in their income statements and balance sheets. The more informed you are, the better prepared you are to sell.

Employee stability

Employees are most company's key assets, so make sure to have a solid team in place before you begin marketing your business. Once you lose a key person or operations manager you will start raising eyebrows during marketing. Employees will not always be with you, so the best time to sell is when key positions have been stable. Nothing scares off a potential buyer faster than a key employee's recent departure.

Cash Flow

It might not be an overstatement to say that in buying and selling small businesses, "Cash flow is everything." When cash flow is not "everything" is when the assets are the only value of the company or if a competitor is just looking at your customer base. If cash flow has started to slide and you are thinking about selling, there is serious work to do. A Band-Aid will not work. You will need to get to the heart of the problem and get the problem handled.

When reviewing a business, prospective buyers and lenders key in on even the slightest slip in annual revenue or cash flow. Even an annual dip as small as 2% will cause a buyer or lender to wonder if there are significant problems in the business. We have sold businesses with a drop in cash flow for two and three consecutive years, but the final sale price negotiated suffered as a result.

4

The Marketing Package
Gathering the Right Documents

When studying for a big final exam, attending study groups, preparing classroom notes and going to the library are keys to success. The same is true for one of life's biggest exams – selling a business. Having all the pertinent documents ready for the sale will shorten the amount of time it takes to garner the greatest number of qualified buyers and to attain the highest justifiable price. Without all the pertinent documents, a buyer cannot make an informed purchase decision. The following items are a list of the documents and information needed, at a minimum, to prepare a business for sale.

Interim profit and loss statement and balance sheet
The interim financials will bring a buyer up-to-date on the financial strength of a company since the last completed corporate fiscal year and resulting tax return. Since cash flow trends can change monthly, a buyer cannot rely on dated information. The interim financial information is also necessary for lending institutions and it is a safe bet that financials dated within 60 days of closing will be needed from buyer as well.

Three years of tax returns and income statements
Three years of data will paint a picture of the financial stability of a company. A prospective buyer needs to analyze cash flow and earnings trends to determine the direction the business is heading. It's also useful information to prepare the buyer for any cyclical trends. In addition, buyers need to track and analyze trends in expenses and margins. Even if cash flow is increasing, it does not mean a business is heading in the right direction. Any fluctuations, good or bad, will ultimately be clear with financial data from the past three years.

Current asset list
It is easier to justify a business sale price if assets comprise a significant part of the price. Anything above asset value is goodwill and is more difficult to justify. Comprising an asset list with a total value of the assets at fair market price will create a floor value of a business. It is important not to place individual values on assets, but rather to show a total value. Itemizing individual asset values will encourage the buyer to spend more time questioning the value of each asset rather than focusing on the collection of assets and the overall business. One exception that may require individual asset values be listed exists when outside financing is used. A lender will normally require a fair market value to be placed on all assets over $500. Serial numbers for these assets will also be needed.

Asset and Liabilities
Assets and liabilities listed on a balance sheet can be transferred with the sale or kept by a seller. A buyer needs to know exactly what assets and liabilities are to be transferred with the sale so he can make an educated offer. Samples of these items include: accounts receivable, accounts payable, pre-paid deposits, cash, debt on assets, leases, etc.
By identifying what is included from the start, misunderstandings can be eliminated. It is prudent for a seller to identify which leases and notes can be transferred to the buyer before the negotiating process begins. Discovering a liability that cannot be assumed until late in the process, after the deal has been structured, is inconvenient and could cause a deal to collapse.

Facility information

A prospective buyer wants to know everything about the facility that will house his new business. A few questions the seller should answer are: Where is it located? Is there a long-term lease? Is real estate included in the deal? What is the square footage?

If you are renting, it is crucial to perform preliminary due diligence to determine if the lease can be assumed, how much time is left on the lease and other factors that would impact the business acquisition. Leases are not easy legal instruments to negotiate. The lease can be a deal stopper if attention is not paid to this area from the beginning. Most owners do not want to involve their landlords in the sale process until they know that the deal is going to go through. If the landlord may be difficult or want to change the lease term or rate to the buyer, it is a good idea to know what the new parameters will be before negotiations start. If a landlord desires a longer lease than a buyer wants, a lease option to extend after the base period rather than a fixed long-term commitment might be an option.

If you own the real estate and will be leasing it to the buyer, it is important to determine any trends effecting building taxes and insurance. Those should be addressed in the lease. It is important to determine the rent you would charge a new owner since it will have an impact on his cash flow. If you own the real estate and plan to increase the lease amount, be aware that this added amount will be subtracted from the cash flow, resulting in a lower business sale price. Often the lease amount can be structured to remain constant for the first two or three years. A delayed increase may not lower the sale price the same way an immediate increase will. Again, awareness of these factors before the process begins gives you a stronger negotiating position.

Employee information

The most valuable asset in addition to FF& E (Furniture, Fixtures and Equipment) is the employee base.

At a minimum, the following questions at should be answered in the information prepared in a marketing package: How many employees are there? What is the tenure of each employee? What is the pay structure? Is the workforce stable? Do the employees know the business is for sale? Is the owner willing to stay on as an employee? Whatever employee information is provided can be displayed by replacing specific names with titles.

An outstanding graphic tool to summarize the employee situation is an organizational chart. The chart should include the following variables: employee hierarchy, tenure, pay, responsibilities, and titles. Because the value placed on employees is a part of goodwill, it is more difficult to validate. The more information provided about employees, the more salable a business will be.

Company history and CBOR
A chronological summary of a business will provide a prospective buyer a road map to a company's history. A prospective buyer will be able to look at historic financial statements together with the company's narrative of the business history to perform an overall analysis.

 Sample of questions to consider are: Has a new line been recently added? Has the business been moved? When was this business formed? Is the business run by the original owner? What marketing plans and efforts have been done since the company's beginning? A CBOR (Confidential Business Review) will be completed by the seller with assistance from Peterson Acquisitions to showcase the details of the business and the opportunity for the buyer or soon to be new owner.

Other information to include:
Asking Price – Must be reasonable and fair to both seller and buyer.
Deal Structure and Financing – Is owner financing a consideration? Does this company have the potential for SBA financing? If so, what are the terms?
Marketing Strategies – Is there an opportunity to improve cash flow through a more aggressive marketing campaign?
Reason for selling?- Is the seller retiring, is there a divorce, is he burned out, etc?

Industry Trends – How are revenues trending in the industry as a whole? Is there a consolidation movement within this industry?

Industry Trade Journal – In most cases, a buyer will not have industry experience. A seller can recommend trade journals a prospective buyer can access to learn. . If certain articles from past issues point to a healthy industry outlook, make copies and distribute them to buyers. *Published articles* – Has the business been featured in a newspaper article? Has the owner or one of the employees written a trade article?

5

The Heart of the Matter
Understanding Cash Flow

Numbers talk, B.S walks

Honest and verifiable cash flow will greatly impact the sale price of a small business. Many buyers and business brokers go as far as stating that cash flow is everything. More than 70% of small business buyers are first time buyers coming out of corporate America. These buyers have one primary goal – to replace the income stream they lost coming out of their former jobs. For these buyers, the owner's cash flow, secured through the small business acquisition, is their salvation and their main decision point on company value.

What is Owners Cash Flow (CASH FLOW)? The simplest definition is: The amount of money a new owner would be able to take out of the business annually or the net benefit to the owner.

Through financial analysis, most CASH FLOW items are fairly easy to quantify, such as net profit and owner's salary. Some of the figures may be somewhat more difficult to discern. A professional business broker can assist in recasting the business' income statement to determine CASH FLOW. A business broker's job is not to create cash flow, but to be able to substantiate what is documented through company financials, tax returns, and a due diligence process. The following are the most common elements that comprise CASH FLOW.

Net Income
Net Income before income taxes is the amount leftover after all expenses are deducted from revenue or the amount on which federal taxes are based. The net income can fluctuate from more than the normal increases and decreases in revenues and expenses. A good accountant will attempt to keep net income as low as possible for tax purposes; therefore, small net income does not necessarily reflect an unprofitable business. For example, a business owner might prepay expenses toward the end of a year in order to push tax liabilities to the following year if his net income is projected to be too high.

Owner Salary
The amount of owner salary is normally a large component of CASH FLOW. Similar to net income, the amount of owner's salary may fluctuate for tax purpose. When a business owner receives a salary, he has to pay taxes as an employer and employee; therefore, many times business owners elect to be paid a smaller salary and pay themselves through owner perks or net income.

Depreciation / Amortization
Depreciation and amortization is a component of CASH FLOW. Both are non-cash expenses used to reduce taxes. Depreciation decreases taxable income but does not reduce cash. Lending institutions include depreciation and amortization in their cash flow calculations.

Interest expense

Interest is a component of CASH FLOW since it directly relates to the amount of funding of a particular owner rather than the business. A new owner might have more capital and therefore may not need financing, reducing interest expenses to zero. Interest can be attributable to bank loans, personal loans, equipment leases or any other debt instrument. Interest may go away after the sale.

Non-recurring expenses

One-time or non-recurring expenses can be considered components of CASH FLOW. In the most recently completed corporate tax year, determine whether an expense was non-recurring or extraordinary. The amount identified can be added to CASH FLOW. Extraordinary litigation expense is a good example unless litigation is an annual occurrence. Even uncollectible accounts receivable that are above the norm can most often be included

Owner perks

One of the benefits of owning a small business is the ability to have a business pay for certain personal expenses. Owner perks are expenses that are personal to the owner; therefore none of these costs would be transferred to the new owner. If you have a paper trail of the owner perks, a buyer may then consider them in his analysis of sale price. The most common owner perks that are acceptable by a prospective buyer are:

Car Payment payment	Spouse and children's car
Car insurance insurance	Spouse and children's car
Health Insurance insurance	Spouse and children's health
Life Insurance	Spouse's life insurance
401(k) contributions	charitable contributions
IRA	Meals and entertainment
Travel and Entertainment	

Below is an example of a calculation of CASH FLOW:

Net income	$100,000
Depreciation	$ 50,000
Interest	$ 20,000
Owner Salary	$ 80,000
Owner travel (personal)	$ 5,000
Owner auto (personal)	$ 6,000
Owner health insurance	$7,000
Owners Cash Flow	$268,000

A word of caution about including owner perks in the CASH FLOW analysis to justify a selling price: if a business is being sold with mostly owner financing, all of the verifiable owner perks can be used. If the business will be financed through SBA or a conventional bank, financial institutions will vary as to what will be accepted as legitimate CASH FLOW. A lending institution considers primarily adjusted EBITDA (Earnings before Interest, Depreciation, and Amortization) plus owner's salary, when they calculate their debt coverage analysis to determine if they will fund.

6

What is Your Business Worth?
Understanding the Valuation Process

Placing a market value on a business will be the most important part of the selling process. Business owners usually have misconceptions concerning the value of their business. Most of the time, a buyer believes his business is worth more than a realistic valuation will determine.

Prospective buyers make the decision to purchase a business based on the future upside potential, but will establish a price on the business based on past and current performance. Fortunately, performance is well documented in company financial reports from which a business valuator can use definitive ratios to determine net worth. There are probably as many formulas to develop market value as there are different types of businesses. In the final analysis, there is one definitive determinant of business worth: "The amount a willing and educated buyer is willing to pay for a business."

When you are ready to begin the valuation process, remember that a business broker or a business valuation service is the best bet in determining a value that is in line with what a buyer is willing to pay for the business. A professional business broker is in the marketplace working with buyers. His finger is on the pulse of market conditions that affect values. The worst thing a seller can do is to listen to others' opinions about market value. A business broker will confer with the seller's CPA. The business broker will then use comparable business cash flow, financial information and present market conditions to determine market value.

Cash flow

The largest component of determining value is deciphering how much money the business makes. Different valuation methods give cash flow many different meanings. When dealing with small businesses, the description of Cash Flow (CASH FLOW) will be used in most valuation models. A detailed description was discussed in the previous chapter. Most small business sale prices are determined by using a multiple of cash flow. If a prospective buyer cannot receive a good return on his investment for a business purchase, the business price is too high. If the business is purchased using leverage and the CASH FLOW cannot cover the debt payment, the business is likely overpriced and will probably not sell. In real estate, a buyer's main focus is location. In business acquisitions it is CASH FLOW.

Asset value

Many buyers want to know how much of the business price is determined by what they can feel and touch, or hard assets. Normally, the higher the value of the asset, the higher the sale price. Conversely, outdated, non-working duplicate assets do not add value to a company; rather, they detract from it. Just as important as getting a business valuation, getting an equipment appraisal could assist in the valuation of the overall business.

A business owner needs to ensure that his business does not become "upside-down" (his asset value is much higher than his CASH FLOW), since that would yield him a sale price driven primarily by his asset value. Assets are essential to the operation of any business, but if an owner is continually building an asset base and not consequently building the cash flow, he is hindering the ultimate sale price.

Inventory

Inventory value falls under the same heading as assets, which are items a prospective buyer can feel and touch. Inventory, similar to assets, is essential to the operation of a business, yet too much inventory can have a negative effect on sale price as well. A sale price can be determined with or without inventory value, but either method will require an inventory count before the closing date. Dead and obsolete inventory will not add proportionate value since it will not be counted at closing and therefore is deducted from the ultimate sale price.

Accounts Receivable (A/R) and Accounts Payable (A/P)

When a small business is valued, it is normally based on a multiple of cash flow with hard assets and inventory included in the sale price. When A/R and/or AP are included in a business sale, the price derived from the earning multiple will be adjusted up or down based on the net values of the A/R and A/P. Normally, language in the closing docs for any uncollectible A/R either affects the seller carry-back note (if there is one) or a refund of a portion of the sale price. If a seller does not want to hassle with adjusting A/R after closing, a buyer can take a chance on A/R by paying a predetermined discounted percentage.

Conversely, accounts payable decreases the business sale price dollar for dollar. Example: $1,000,000 all cash sale price, $ 800,000 cash at closing, $ 200,000 assumption of A/P.

Asset vs. Stock

Asset Purchases are better for both the buyer and seller as opposed to a stock sale. With an Asset Purchase the buyer assumes no liability or risk from the previous owner whether it is a pending lawsuit or possible actions taken against the owner. It also is advantageous for taxes to sell using an Asset Purchas Agreement versus Stock. A stock purchase is best used for larger or publicly held corporation.

Years in business

Longevity in business equals less risk in the human mind. While it may not be true, dealing with the psychology of people makes it a factor to be aware of. Kodak was one of the largest companies in the United States for many decades. They are no longer in business.

Market trends, new technology and the changing landscape of convenience and advancement in certain industries make some businesses or services extinct. You can't rely on years in business to determine the right business to buy. Look at the market. Since the purchase of a business is one of the hardest decisions one will make, a buyer needs to eliminate as much uncertainty as possible. All things being equal, a fifteen year-old firm will sell more quickly and for more money than a five-year-old firm with similar financials. A good broker can help the buyer make a wise decision at the various cross roads in the acquisition process.

Employees

The saying, "Employees are a company's most important asset," applies more during the business acquisitions process than perhaps any other time. Quality, quantity and tenure of employees will have a direct effect on not only the value of a company, but also on the probability of the business being sold.

 The strength of the employee pool starts at the top with a solid management team and/or a right-hand person. Buyers will be keenly interested in determining which employees will be able to help them learn the business and survive the transition period. Businesses that have the owner as, "chief, cook, and bottle washer" will not command the price and attention of a company with a solid management team in place.

Reason for Selling-It could be anything

A difficult psychological obstacle for any buyer is understanding or believing the seller's reason for selling. A justifiable, acceptable reason for sale will increase the probability of sale for the highest justifiable price.

The top reasons for buyers are retirement, fatigue, and sickness. The most common reason for the seller is probably fatigue, which usually occurs between 7-12 years of ownership, in other words, the owner's shelf life. The least acceptable and most problematic reasons for buyers include: inability to handle the business, preference for another business, or problems with employees.

Length of training

Standard procedure in almost any business acquisition is for the seller to be required to remain with the company for a period of time to train the new owner in the operation of the business. The length of time will vary based in part on how well the owner has distanced himself from the business in the years before the sale. If the seller is the "chief, cook and bottle washer" then it is a safe bet that the transition period will be longer since the seller is the only one with the important knowledge. Similarly, if the business is technical and dependent upon the owner in the operation, the training will likely last for an extended period. In any other circumstance, the training period will likely be only a month or two. Usually, this short period is at no cost to the new owner. It is important to remember that some buyers will want the seller out of the operation as soon as possible. They want to be able to fully assert themselves in their new role. Conversely, other buyers want to keep the seller around for as long as possible as a safety net. It is good procedure to structure additional time after the original period for phone consultation or monthly meetings. This additional consultation period adds a comfort level to the new owner and will often shorten the time the seller might otherwise be needed or expected to stay.

Customer and supplier base allocation

"Don't put all your eggs in one basket" applies similarly to the customer and supplier base. If one or two customers account for a majority of the business, it might be easier to operate, but it could have a negative effect on the sale price. As a general rule, a company should not have one customer represent more than 15% of the company's total cash flow. Buyers are concerned with the possibility of losing one or two large customers. They perceive it as an inherent weakness they would rather not risk.

Having a limited base of suppliers not only poses an inherent risk, but it also limits the ability to provide a wide range of products and services. Buyers are aware that a one supplier may be tied to the company based largely on the supplier's relationship with the owner, who is leaving. A diversified customer and supplier base spreads out risk and eliminates the concern of losing those all-important one or two customers and/or suppliers.

Business type

Some people prefer a Chevy to a Ford, or a two-story home to a ranch style home. There are different buyer preferences for business types as well.

Some types of businesses are more attractive than others to prospective buyers. A manufacturing buyer would not be comfortable behind the counter in a retail store and vice versa. There is a well-defined hierarchy of desirability in the different types of businesses. The four primary types of businesses listed in order of desirability are: Manufacturing, Wholesale, Service and Retail.

Additional factors that may increase or decrease a company's market value:

Market Strength – Does the business have a strong market share in the industry?

Industry growth – Is the business in a growing industry?

Appearance – Does the business show well? Is it clean? Is there enough space? What would it cost to remodel or redefine the business?

Location – Is the business in a major city? Is it easy to get to?

Owner's involvement – Is the owner the whole business? Does the owner work 100 hours per week?

7

Should you do it on your own?
Why use a Business Broker?

The right representation can make the difference between closing or losing a deal. Due to confidentiality, a business broker cannot simply place a sign in a window like a real estate broker and wait for a prospective buyer to call. A professional business broker finds financially capable prospects, negotiates the deal and sets up closing without anyone finding out until the deal is done.

Pricing a business

How can a seller be sure the price set is the highest justifiable price? Does the price enables a seller, to receive the highest price the market will pay without leaving money on the table? A competent business broker will be able to help the seller arrive at this price. Having a business on the market at a sale price that is too high will ultimately frighten prospective buyers. Under pricing a business could make the buyer question the worth of the business and cost the seller money. A business broker can assist in determining the best price for taking a business to the market.

Buyer prospecting

Once a business owner decides to sell his business and all the pertinent documents have been prepared, how will prospective buyers find out about the business? How can the seller be assured a buyers is capable? A majority of people in the United States have thought about owning their own business but only a small percentage ever do. On average, for every prospective buyer introduced to a business owner, a broker has usually met with between 10-30 prospects. Many want-to-be buyers do not have the financial resources, are not a good fit or are just "tire kicking". A business broker will act as a buffer and allow the seller to concentrate on running the business rather than wasting valuable time, jacking around with unqualified buyers.

Confidentiality

Preserving confidentiality is one of the main reasons to hire a business broker. A professional business broker will have variations of confidentiality agreements drawn up and waiting for a prospective buyer. The broker is familiar effectively administering this important document. Most business brokers will not discuss a business with a perspective buyer unless a confidentiality agreement has been signed. To further ensure confidentiality, a financial statement from the buyer will often be required at the same time the confidentiality agreement is signed. The idea is that if a prospect signs both a confidentiality agreement and gives his financial statement, he will most likely adhere to confidentiality and not waste time kicking tires. These measures are taken in the beginning, before a company name or location is given.

Higher sale price

There are several skill sets a professional business broker uses to ensure that a seller gets the right price for a business. Evaluation experience, market awareness, and knowledge of deal structure are a few of these skills.

A business broker sells businesses daily and is knowledgeable about current supply and demand. No other professional is in this position. It is important to use everyone on a support team for their specific area of expertise. Refer to your attorney to draft legal documents, your CPA for his tax advice, and your broker to guide you through the business acquisition process.

The business broker draws on his and the sellers positions of strength to obtain the highest justifiable price. Having knowledge of comparable cash flow and active business offerings enables the business broker to position buyers more effectively. The business broker does not work directly for the business but rather as a consultant, which allows him to negotiate with prospects unemotionally.

Negotiating a better deal

The old adage, "You cannot negotiate the best deal for yourself" certainly applies when trying to sell a business. Do you do your own dental work? Cut your own hair? Here is the problem: A business owner is emotionally tied to his business and negotiates on emotion rather than reason. A business broker can negotiate for the owner because he is not connected with emotion to the business. The broker's emotional interest is in operating in the owner's best interests. A business broker has dealt with many business acquisitions and is aware of all the pain-in-the-ass issues that can come up. He can weather those storms with detachment. A seller often cannot. A broker foresees problems and deals with them, while a business owner going through the process for the first time could lose a deal because of an emotional reaction, sending the deal to down the drain.

Professional marketing program

An experienced business owner certainly knows how to run a successful entity and make it grow.

When you are ready to sell, the "nuts and bolts" of your business have to be presented in the most honest and positive manner in order to entice prospective buyers to consider your business as an acquisitions candidate. A business broker is skilled at preparing concise, powerful marketing packages on businesses he represents. After a package has been prepared, going to market like an 800 pound Gorilla is the only way to win. You must be voracious if you want a victory. Without a proper marketing campaign, an otherwise terrific business may go unnoticed.

Most business brokers will search their internal database for pre-qualified buyers to find a match for your business. If no match is found, a business broker will use marketing mediums such as newspaper, internet, trade publications, and other business brokerage firms until the right buyer is discovered. Even though a business broker utilizes an enormous amount of time, effort, and money to market a business, it is a fraction of what an owner would expend. A business broker knows the quickest, most effective methods of reaching the best buyers for this particular business, while preserving confidentiality.

The closing process

The closing process is usually the most strenuous and nerve racking step for all parties involved. A seasoned business broker experienced the process many times. The broker will have worked with a variety of closing attorneys or escrow companies. He will be able to handle the problems that arise with them. The business broker, along with the closer, will ensure that the seller's interest is protected and that the deal goes through.

Handling the support team

Having a support team in place to facilitate the process is important. Your CPA, attorney, broker, lender, comptroller, and others will be needed in the process. It is crucial to have a point person to coordinate the team. That person should be your business broker.

Using a business broker to sell your business will alleviate the time constraints involved in coordinating your support team. Most importantly, no one on your team will have the experience that a business broker has. Members of the team specialize in different areas, but the business broker is the only one whose job is to facilitate and coordinate the entire process.

Business broker services

Following is a list of services that a qualified business broker provides during the business acquisitions process:

Consultation with seller and review of seller's documentation
Review of seller's financial statements

Preparation of a listing agreement, seller's disclosure, and seller file

Development and marketing package

Initial buyer response interview and screening

Business Showings and buyer follow-up

Additional consultations with buyer/seller

Assisting buyer with preparation of Offer to Purchase or Letter of Intent and presentation to seller

Meetings with buyer/seller to coordinate buyer due diligence

Consultations with buyer/seller and outside advisors

Coordination of closing and other documentations

Consultation with parties regarding acquisitions of licenses, utilities, etc.

8

Choosing the Right Business Broker

Choose a business broker who is responsive, able to answer questions, and produces buyers, arranges meetings and pushes for an offer.. Choose someone who is passionate about serving you, not just a guy trying to make a deal regardless of whether or not it is good for the buyer and seller. Otherwise you are wasting your time

Business experience

Unless a business broker has "walked in your shoes," he can never fully understand what a seller will go through emotionally or psychologically. While there may be successful business brokers who have never sat in an owner's chair, prior ownership experience adds an important element that can make a difference. Business brokers with prior business ownership experience have boots on the ground knowledge of the emotional struggles of running and selling a business.

Understanding cash flow and sale price analysis

A business broker must be able to analyze financial statements to determine cash flow since it is the method that helps determine the sale price. This calculation is usually done in the first or second meeting with a seller.

Normally, a business owner will not list his business with a business broker until the cash flow is completed and understood by the seller. This would be an outstanding screening point to determine if the business broker is right for you. Ask the business broker to explain the formula and analysis used to determine the market value of your business. Listen carefully to the explanation, since this will be the same rationale given to prospective buyers. An experienced business broker will be able to clearly and convincingly explain his thought process. Be leery of business brokers who will market a business for the price a business owner suggests based on needs or wants, rather than calculations based on the financials and market analysis.

Analysis of deal structure
A good business broker should explain and present choices of structure. In determining deal structure, has the business broker asked you what you want to achieve in selling? He should ask what you need in cash at closing or what kind of income stream you want and for how long. Although a seller's needs do not set the final sale price, the business broker should have enough awareness to ask you these questions. He should offer you choices of deal structure. All cash, owner financing, conventional financing, SBA, or a combination of bank and seller financing are examples of structure. These functions alone can be the difference between success, failure, gain, or average profit in selling.

Marketing plan
The   marketing plan and package are the channels that reach prospective buyers. It is essential that a business broker be able to prepare and distribute a plan to the right prospects.
The analysis should be coherent and easy to understand since it will be given to prospective buyers. Is the cash flow analysis, sales price formula and deal structure understandable in the marketing plan? If the marketing package consists only of a one or two page prospectus on the business, how can a buyer gain the understanding of the business they need to make a good decision?

Is there advertising in the local or national newspapers or trade publications as a normal course of business? In short, what is the plan to reach the most qualified buyers with the highest level of confidentiality? Does the business broker have his own web site? If so, visit it to learn more about his business before you have the first meeting.

Buyer profiling

In the same meeting that the business broker analyzes cash flow and deal structure, buyer profiling should be discussed. If the business broker suggests that the buyer will come from corporate America and you want all cash, he should discuss SBA financing as an option and explain why your deal would fit their parameters. A good business broker should be able to do more than just present buyers; he should find qualified buyers that fit financially and who can make a decision and move forward quickly.

Confidentiality

The issue of confidentiality should be a focal topic in the first discussion you have with a business broker. He should explain why it is important and specifically how he intends to handle the issue. Does he have a buyer profile form that asks questions about the buyer's financial requirements and professional background? Since it is necessary to perform a more thorough professional background check if you are going to have owner financing, does the business broker have the tools to facilitate this check? Determine at what point the business broker obtains the buyer's financial statements and credit report.

References

Business owners are guarded about giving out information about selling their business. They have employees, competition and many other people and things to consider and a business to protect. That is why a good broker is extremely discreet with any information he obtains from the seller. It is also why a prospective buyer signs an NDA (non-disclosure agreement) and gives the broker his own financial information.

A buyer worthy of the trust both buyers and sellers place in him will not share information or references about businesses he has sold in the past.

9

Walking the Emotional Tightrope
Who are the Buyers?

Where will you find buyers? You will have a head start if you can
identify the most likely type of buyer in advance. A few questions to
consider while identifying possible buyers are: Will the buyer have
industry experience? Will he be a first time buyer? Will he need
financing? By answering these questions, a seller will be able to
forecast the buyer's probable financing needs and list of priorities.

Corporate executive
70% of the buyers for small businesses are first time buyers. Most of
them come out of corporate America. This type of buyer generally
needs some type of financing and is usually either a victim of
corporate downsizing or will have voluntarily opted out of the
corporate rat race. What determines the business he ultimately
purchases will decided by a combination of factors including good
cash flow, location and availability.

Geography is sometimes as important to a displaced executive as financing. He will typically own a home and be unwilling to relocate since the financial benefits of the deal are usually not large enough to allow for, or justify relocation. He wants to replace his recently lost salary with a similar income from his new· company. The executive buyer will usually have a quick time frame to choose a business since he will generally not have the financial resources for a down payment in addition to maintaining his living expenses over an extended period. The corporate executive is looking for a "job" to buy and a small business affords him that opportunity. This type buyer usually has a professional resume, college degree, and good credit, making him a candidate for SBA financing which will afford a seller the maximum amount of cash at closing.

A word of caution about buyers who are still employed in corporate America. They are rarely in a position to make a quick decision, if any decision at all. Often the employed executive is waiting to uncover the business of his dreams and then will decide if he is really going to give entrepreneurism a try. Be cautious with a corporate buyer. He may very well be a dreamer rather than a doer.

Competitors

Due to confidentiality, competitors/vendors should be approached with caution. They should be the last prospects to approach. With all due respect to signed confidentiality agreements, by marketing your business you are exposing yourself to people in position to harm you in the marketplace. You should keep your cards close to your vest regarding company information if you do talk to a competitor or vendor

There are some advantages, however, in selling to either competitors or vendors. The decision process and due diligence period can be shortened since the acquiring company knows the market and the industry. These buyers are often only interested in verifying basic company information and determining if there is a synergistic fit. In addition, financing difficulties are not as prevalent as with other types of buyers. The seller may not be required to offer any form of owner financing since the acquiring company may have that basis covered from the beginning.

Most often in our experience, business-to-business purchasers are not the highest paying buyers because they are unwilling to pay the highest justifiable price for a business. Often these buyers would rather set up their own facility with in-house assets rather than pay top price for an ongoing concern that includes substantial goodwill value. Many times, owners with dollar signs in their eyes visualize selling to a large company with deep pockets in their industry. Although this situation has certainly occurred, especially during consolidation periods in an industry, it is not the norm.

Existing employees

Many business owners feel that the best prospect for their business will be within the employee ranks. This can be a viable, possibility. Several sellers have requested that we present their business to the key employees before taking it to the general market. It is normal to think that employees would be a natural choice, but there is a saying about people in business: "There are Chiefs, and there are Indians; very few Indians ever become Chiefs." After an employee and his spouse discover the reality of the down payment, the monthly debt payments, and the overall responsibilities involved in ownership, the employee usually chooses to remain an "Indian." Selling to employees presents another challenge: it is likely of the owner will feel or be made to feel obligated to provide some form of owner financing and working capital. In the event the new employee-turned-owner runs into financial hardship, the seller may find himself in a tough situation.

Investment groups

Investment groups are always lurking in the shadows for good deals. These buyers are going to be interested in both a superior investment and a strong management infrastructure. In many instances, the investment group has no interest in running the business themselves and is only interested in the cash flow. In this situation, the seller may be in good position to stay on as a manager while receiving an income stream from the sale. It is safe to say that if a business does not have capable management in place, the investment group will not be interested or will drastically discount the deal.

10

First Impressions
Working with Buyers

The best advice available on the subject of buyer relations is to exercise patience and understanding. If the relationship between a buyer and seller gets sideways, the deal may be doomed. The transaction may still close, but continued animosity could have a negative effect on sale price and the overall deal. Let's not forget, after closing buyer and seller will still have to work together during the transition period.

Emotions
In many instances, the larger the transaction, the better the relationship between the buyer and seller. In our experience, smaller deals seem to have more emotion involved. Our smallest and simplest deals see the principals get into heated negotiations early in the transaction. It greatly complicates the situation and frustrates everyone involved. This can make for hard-to-close transactions or, worse, lost deals.

The seller is emotional because the business that is up for sale is his "baby". The buyer is emotional because he is buying his future in what is probably the biggest transaction of his life. Emotionally backed transactions are frequently a tight rope.   The best antidote for this potential trauma is for each side to constantly place themselves in the other's shoes.

Picking the right buyer

Most buyers coming out of corporate America will have a professional resume, which can be examined to determine if his experience will be beneficial in running your business. In addition, you'll want to check personal financial statements.

Regardless of the method of financing, the buyer will be required to have a substantial down payment. Most likely, the buyer will need more money to get into your business than you had when you started. Having the required funding does not guarantee a buyer will be a good prospect but it does minimize the risk. If a buyer invests the resources necessary to make a significant initial injection and, in addition, has working capital, you can be assured that he will do everything it takes to maintain the success of the company.

The usual process of selling will involve some sort of get acquainted meeting between buyer and seller. Expect the buyer to ask most of the questions in these initial meetings. As a seller, you have already disclosed much proprietary and financial information on your business. This is a good time to get additional information from a buyer. In addition to a resume and credit check, it is a good idea for the owner to ask the buyer what plans he would have for the business. This may be a hard question for a buyer to answer since he really does not know the business, but how he responds can reveal why he thinks the business is a good fit.

His ideas and answers can help you determine if this is a prospect with whom you want to work. If you have a good feel for the buyer, you are in a much better position to negotiate the sale.

Timely information requests

During the acquisitions process there will be a continuing demand to supply the buyer with information. The requests may seem never ending. Your support team (CPA, business broker, etc.) cannot forecast every possible document that will be required or requested, since every deal is different. Copies of all leases and notes to be assumed may be needed. Various accounts receivable and payable reports may need to be updated. Therefore, a seller should be poised at all times to get the information needed to the buyer in an expedient manner.

11

One Shot, One Bullet
Showing a Business

Showing a business is mostly about perception. The showing is more than just touring a prospective buyer through the building and showing him four walls and a new paint job. A proper showing can leave a buyer with the perception of a well-organized, organizational structure capable of continuing to be profitable.

Business appearance

Most business showings are performed after business hours due to confidentiality. The buyer should understand that employees may be unaware of a possible sale until the acquisitions process is almost complete.

In preparing a business for sale, look at the business from a buyer's perspective. From the outside, does the parking lot look as though attention has been paid to orderly parking arrangement and traffic flow? Does the company sign outside project a thriving concern? Or is it, as we have seen many times, an old sign that needs painting or neon with letters missing --probably for months. Some thriving businesses do not have a sign at all. Remember the key: place yourself in the buyer's shoes.

A showing will be the first time the buyer sees a business, even if he has seen it every day for years. This will be the first time he sees it with intent to purchase. The important point is that a buyer's perception starts with his first external impression.

Internal business appearance
How does your entrance look? About half the entrance halls or waiting rooms we have seen need new carpet, furniture, or new paint. The appearance of a business can give the impression of organization or disorganization. Floors should be swept, employee's desks should be neat at the end of each business day and equipment should always be clean. A buyer's visit will always be announced in advance, allowing you ample time to clean, organize and be ready for a showing.

Warehouse layout
Warehouse shelving for products should be numbered and neatly laid out. Nothing is more bewildering to a buyer than looking at row after row of products without any numbers or designations that identify them. As the owner, you may have looked at these items for years and know exactly where to find whatever you might be need at any moment. You are very comfortable with the layout and structure. Will the buyer be?
Everything should be in its place and well organized. It's all about efficiency and ergonomics in work flow.

Website
Another item that can help show a business is a company website. Having a good website gives the buyer the perception of a progressive company that has joined the technological wave, one that is still looking for potential customers.

12

What Do You Want to Achieve?
Negotiating and Deal Structure

Every business acquisition will involve some form of negotiations before the process is ultimately finalized. The negotiating phase can be arduous. The final result may be radically different from the original deal. If a business owner is not prepared to properly negotiate, he could lose a deal or settle for a lesser deal and not even realize it. The best deal does not always constitute the highest price. The deal structure is always part of the negotiations. From all-cash transactions to owner-financed deals, remember that deal structure is a major factor of negotiation. The following are negotiating point—besides the sale price-- that can be used to obtain the best overall deal.

Allocation of sale price
Allocation of sale price is just as important as the sale price itself. It determines how the sale price will be divided.

Many owners spend weeks negotiating the sale price without considering the tax implications of the allocation of the price. Minor concessions on the sale price can be compensated through the allocation process. An awareness and understanding of the allocation areas and their respective implications to both parties will give the seller an advantage in the negotiating process. It is a good idea to go over these allocation areas with your CPA and determine the potential tax implications from the beginning. Some allocation areas include fixed assets, goodwill, consulting, non-compete agreements, employment contracts, and real estate. The allocation of sale price should be reviewed between the seller and his CPA before the process starts to determine the best mix of variables that constitute the best sale price.

Taxes

Owners are often unprepared for the ultimate tax implications of the sale of their business. We have seen business owners attempt to change deal structure well into negotiations when they discover their tax liability and realize they cannot stomach the deal they have negotiated. In fact, promising deals that were ready to close failed to do so because the seller had not prepared himself in this area. It is crucial to get a CPA involved early to fully understand the tax liabilities and avoid paying a majority of the sale price to Uncle Sam. Depending on the corporate structure (C-Corp, S-Corp, LLP, etc) there can be many tax advantages and/or disadvantages for structuring each individual deal a certain way.

Handling assets and liabilities

Which balance sheet items can be assumed by a new owner? It is beneficial to know before beginning the business acquisitions process.

Many sellers are concerned about bringing creditors into the picture until they know that they have a firm deal. Since buyers can bring only a certain amount of liquidity to the table, assuming balance sheet items can allow a buyer to purchase your business with less cash out of pocket. That warrants a higher sale price. For example, regardless of the type of financing, you may or may not elect to sell the Accounts Receivable (A/R) and/or Accounts Payable (A/R). These variables provide negotiating points for any transaction. If it is decided to include both, the net balance between these two values will either add to or subtract from the overall sale price at closing.

Earn out

An earn-out provision is a tool that can overcome a deadlock on sale price negotiations. An earn out basically provides that in a specified number of years after the sale, if cash flow (or gross profit for example) stays the same as at the time of sale, the seller gets 100% payment on the owner note. If cash flow drops by a certain percentage, the owner note is likewise reduced by that same percentage. Usually, there is not a corresponding increase to the seller on note payment if the cash flow increases, since that increase will be the result of the buyer's efforts. A seller can take the position that there is only downside risk to him, but earn-out is used to handle only the amount of sale price that is in dispute, not the total sale price.

Asset vs. Stock

Some deals never reach the negotiating stage because the seller wants to sell stock instead of assets. In many of these situations, the seller has been given preliminary information that he has to sell stock or else it would be a bad deal for him. A CPA and an attorney that specialize in business acquisitions will assist a seller through this area. Almost always, buyers want to purchase the assets of a corporation because of tax and liability issues.

Selling a company with an asset basis and still benefiting tax wise puts a seller in a strong negotiating position. If a seller will only consider selling the stock and that's it, the deal may end before it starts. A seller needs to know the tax implications of both sides of the deal. As mentioned, a key to successful negotiating is to obtain specialized help before starting the selling process.

Non-compete agreements

Though not a major negotiation point, non-compete agreements can be used in the negotiation process. Most buyers are concerned about a seller's ability to return to the industry and compete against them. A non-compete agreement reduces a buyer's concern and disallows a seller's ability to return to the industry. A non-compete agreement could have many negotiating points including the length of time, distance parameters, and range of industry positions.

Length of training

Although training is not a major negotiating point, it can be used as one. One or two months of seller training are normally all that is required in the sale, especially if phone consultation for a nominal period follows. If you are close on sale price, you can always adjust the length of training and even charge for it to compensate.

Earnest money

Some business owners falsely believe that earnest money is some form of guarantee. They treat it as an area for hard negotiation. Actually, the amount placed on deposit by the buyer is only a gesture of good faith. As a seller, time and expense will usually far outweigh the escrow monies received if the deal does not close. If the earnest deposit is viewed as a good faith gesture rather than a negotiating point, it will not be an issue in the deal.

There is no set formula to determine the optimum amount of escrow money that accompanies a purchase contract. Escrow deposits are not a guarantee that a transaction will close. The deposit is refunded to the buyer if he withdraws before the due diligence period. After the buyer has completed his due diligence, the escrow.

Deal structure

Conventional Financing - commonly referred to as "asset based lending." Conventional financing institutions rarely look beyond asset value; therefore, do not consider one of the biggest assets you have to sell, goodwill, as part of their calculations. With conventional financing, lenders do not place a value on goodwill and even worse, place a deeply discounted value on assets. Anyone who has tried to obtain a conventional bank loan with a major portion of the value in goodwill can recall the stringent policies they have in place.

Conventional banks are outstanding sources of funds for lines of credit, real estate, and asset based financing. In the small business arena, conventional financing is not normally available to a buyer unless he has personal assets to collateralize the loan or the sale price is made entirely of asset value. Conventional banks have, at times, helped us all during our business ownership and it is unfair to paint a negative picture, but chances are a buyer will not be able to use conventional financing as a vehicle to purchase a business unless it is heavily asset based and the buyer has collateral to cover the loan.

SBA Financing - At this time, the Small Business Administration (SBA) is an outstanding alternative for financing small businesses. This is a federal agency that will guarantee a portion of an approved loan. This guarantee allows funding for, among other things, goodwill. The SBA focuses just as much on cash flow as they do on assets to approve a loan. The SBA looks at cash flow somewhat differently than the CASH FLOW we discussed earlier in this book. The challenge of obtaining an SBA loan involves the need for a business not only to produce a strong cash flow, but to also have the components of cash flow in the right place. They only take into account EBITDA and owner's salary, with very few, if any, owner perks added to the cash flow. The SBA uses very well defined debt- coverage ratios to ensure a borrower will be able to repay the loan, pay himself a salary and to have enough money left over for contingencies. It is well worth the effort to thoroughly analyze the SBA as an option and determine if your business would qualify for this type of financing vehicle. Generally speaking, the sale price on SBA deals will not be as high as owner financing, but if a business qualifies, this may be an alternative. The seller may have to carry a small owner note, usually not exceeding 5% to 10%, excluding closing costs. The seller would net 90% to 95% of the sale price at closing. Not all business brokers are well versed in SBA transactions so this alternative should be discussed with a business broker before listing the business. Be sure the broker has SBA contacts who aggressively utilize this financing tool.

Owner Financing

Besides bank financing and an all cash transaction, there is the topic of owner financing. Most owners do not want any part of owner financing, mostly because of misconceptions. However, if the business is not suitable for institutional financing, unless they want to discount the business 40% for an all cash transaction, the owner has only two alternatives: Do not sell or owner finance the business.

Owner financing can be an outstanding means of selling to the right buyer. This method of financing can spread out taxes and create an income stream. Taxes are saved since the payout is spread over a number of years, reducing the tax rate over time. An income stream can be assured for several years with an owner receiving an interest rate that is normally higher than a comparable savings or investment. The concerns surrounding owner financing are very real. There are horror stories about owner financing and sellers often only hear one side. If a buyer goes "belly up" on a deal, what are the options? The business might be the only security and a seller could end up getting back a bankrupt business with no inventory, assets, crew or customers. If the deal is structured properly, the seller's note could be collateralized with more than just the business with items such as: securities, a personal guarantee, and other tangible assets. Looking around at successful businesses today, a vast number of them were obtained through owner financing. They were obviously good risks for the seller. The obvious trick in owner financing is picking the right buyer.

Some form of owner note is negotiated in most business acquisitions. Term length, interest rate, and security for the note all come into play in the negotiating process. Most sellers want their money as quickly as possible while the purchaser is concerned about keeping his debt service low. Sellers would be well advised to beware a buyer whose main concern is getting all of his money in the beginning stages of new ownership. Keeping the debt service low, at least in the beginning, helps to aid his buyer's success with his 'baby'.

Fortunately, there are alternatives that can handle concerns on both sides. For example, if term length is a a problem, structuring a long-term loan with equity bumps along the way after the first few years can solve the problems on both sides. Balloon payments can be a good negotiating point. For example, a fifteen -year note with a six year balloon payment is a good compromise. The buyer gets the advantage of lower debt service on the longer note structure in the all-important first few years and the seller gets all of his money earlier with the balloon payment. Similarly, if interest rates become an issue, adding another year of amortization at the agreed interest rate could please both sides.

In summation, there are many ways to negotiate a good deal. There are many ways to successfully resolve issues. The competent negotiator is unemotional, open minded, and fully understands the position of both sides at all times.

13

Reaping the Benefits
Closing

The closing is the best part of the business acquisitions process. You get paid and the complex, sometimes emotionally process ends. If highly trained professionals handle the closing, the process is seamless and quick. If your team is skilled in the arena, they can deal with emotions at the closing table from both the buyer and seller and remain calm through the entire process, even if unexpected events arise. Using an escrow company to handle the closing is the best avenue since they act as a neutral site and work for both the buyer and seller with no bias.

Escrow Company

When selling you need to obtain specialized help. The closing process is no exception. We strongly recommend that an escrow company or an attorney's escrow account be used to close a transaction.

Following are some words of guidance: either the seller's attorney or the buyer's attorney will want to close the deal in his office. If a lender is involved in the business acquisition, the lender will normally require a third party to close and disburse funds. While the parties involved may want to control the closing in their offices, this is exactly what the lender may want to prevent. There are several reasons for this: convenience, control, and the expense incurred by attorneys who make more money by drafting closing documents and spending time at a closing.

The seller's attorney should help prepare and review all the pertinent closing documents prior to closing but should allow an escrow company to handle the actual closing. Make sure the escrow company and attorney coordinate early in the proceedings regarding who will prepare what documents. Getting them both involved early in the process will alleviate problems and delays at closing. If real estate is involved with the acquisitions, the escrow company will also be able to handle that transaction; they will simply get a title company to perform the title search and provide the title policy to be used in closing

Neutral site

Even the best closings we have been part of have often been filled with tension, In many cases, the parties sitting at the closing table have baggage left over from the negotiating process. If for nothing else, the escrow company acts as a neutral site. If the principals have had problems negotiating and hard feelings are prevalent, the escrow company acts as a buffer. The individual assigned to handle the closing does it for a living and will anticipate problems and correct them immediately. These people usually have the acumen and demeanor to handle personalities and tensions. We have seen escrow closers save transactions that the buyer and seller would have lost if there had not been a buffer between them. Many escrow companies have attorneys on staff with support personnel who can edit closing documents at a moment's notice.

Title and lien searches

There is a point in the acquisitions process when the escrow money from the Offer to Purchase or Definitive Agreement is cashed and placed in the escrow company's escrow account. This signifies the opening of escrow and is the point when the escrow company starts performing title and lien searches.

 If real estate is part of the sale, then there needs to be enough time for the escrow company to appoint a title company to perform the title search and prepare the title policy. The additional time is required in the event there is a need to cure title defects or "clouds" with the title and to prepare environmental reports. During the same period the escrow company will also prepare a lien search on the business. Escrow companies often assist in "tying" up loose ends. For example, it is quite common for a paid-off loan to have been improperly filed by the lending institution, and the escrow company will assist in removing the lien from the record. This takes time but is essential to complete the business acquisition. If many pieces of machinery and equipment are being financed, and/or you have numerous loans, liens, or filings on the equipment being conveyed, running a lien search and obtaining approximate payoffs in advance of the closing date will help facilitate the loan closing and help to prevent delays in funding.

Timing

The escrow company will need the signed Offer to Purchase or Definitive Agreement before they can begin preparing the actual closing documents. If leases are being transferred or assigned, the acquisitions documents will also be needed as well as original titles on any vehicles and equipment leases being conveyed. A new lease will need to be given to the escrow company as soon as it is signed.

After they have all of the pertinent documents, many escrow companies can be prepared for closing in a few days. No one can predict how long it will take to prepare documents when working with banks, leasing companies and landlords. The escrow closer assigned to your deal will supply the seller and the buyer with a checklist of the items needed and recommend a timeline for everyone to follow. Simply stated, the closing process is all about getting the documents needed in the correct sequence and in a timely manner. If the simplest of items is missing, closing can and will be delayed.

Closing date

A closing date in the contract of sale should be looked at as a target date only. All parties should be aware that unforeseen events happen. By the time a deal is near closing, there will be numerous parties involved with the transaction. Coordination between everyone and the paper flow usually creates delays. Both the buyer and seller must be flexible. No one can demand a fixed closing date. It is commonplace that a closing date be revised more than once; therefore, patience is the operative word. It is crucial to keep all contracts up to date with any changes to the closing date or other variables to ensure a legal paper trail.

The closing table

There is always a feeling of uncertainty at the closing table. This is the culmination of everyone's efforts and everyone is nervous. This is the final step but the deal can still be lost. If the closing goes well, everyone is happy. If the closing does not go smoothly, the deal will be, at best, delayed.

If the parties involved have done their job preparing the pertinent documents and the deal is in the hands of a professional closer, then relax and enjoy the process. If the SBA or a conventional bank funds the transaction, the process normally takes longer than an all-cash or an owner financed deal. On average, the closing lasts less than an hour. The seller will walk away with a check, copies of all signed documents, and a well-documented closing statement showing all payments and pro-rations. This is the moment of victory for all parties.

14

Murphy's Law
Pitfalls to Avoid

The sale of a business does not have to be marked with problems. We want to identify the most common mistakes that seem to be repeated by business owners who do not have the proper guidance.

Listening to other seller sale prices
Business sales prices have so many variables that comparables are only one of many components. When a business owner discovers that one of his peers sold a business and discovers the sale price, the owner immediately equates that price to his business. The big problem with that logic is that the seller always exaggerates the price of his business and no one ever knows exactly what was included in the sale price.

Overpricing businesses
The ultimate price for a business is the highest justifiable price a buyer will pay for it. The buyer ultimately determines that price, although you need an amount with which to start.

Many business brokers will list a business for sale at whatever price the seller asks--even if the broker knows the price is too high. The broker wants as many listings as possible. An overpriced business will sit on the market and become tarnished over time. By overpricing a business, a seller could lose a good prospect because the prospect thinks that there is not enough leeway to come down in price. If you treat the sale of your business like the sale of a used car, you are in for a long and arduous process. If a business broker is allowed to price a business at the fair market value, the process will be smoother and a seller will ultimately receive the highest justifiable price for his business.

Bad books and records

Many times a business owner "lives" out of his business and his books and records are not kept as well as they should be. A solid, well-run business that has incomplete or inaccurate records will negatively affect the sale price and even prevent a sale. If a buyer needs to obtain outside financing for a business, the inconsistent records could cause a bank to reject a loan. Even worse, a buyer might not feel comfortable enough with the records to place an offer.

Good, clean records are absolutely essential in business acquisitions. If a proper paper trail for revenue and expenses cannot be documented, it is unlikely that the seller will receive his asking price. In fact, one of the biggest reasons deals fail after the contract of sale is signed is due to bad records. If the business is attractive enough, sometimes this won't matter. Remember, market value is what someone is willing to pay for it- regardless of the price tag or what is shown in the books. Stranger things have happened, but don't count on this.

Proving owner perks

The key to effective deal making is the owner's ability to prove cash flow from company financials.

Owner perks, for example, can make up a large portion of a firm's cash flow. If receipts and general ledgers and the connection to the corresponding line item on the P&L statement cannot be traced, the perk should not be included in the cash flow.

Much can be said about owner perks in evaluating a firm's cash flow. The problem is a legality. The IRS has specific guidelines as to what is legally allowed in tax computation. Business owners often walk a fine line in the area of perks. The problem that arises is that in the process of "hiding" the perks, a paper trail is either lost or impossible to reconstruct. There are many profitable businesses that should have sold at much higher prices, but due to poor records or paper trails, the real cash flow could not be established or proven. The company's CPA is often not in a position to assist in the reconstruction of a perk, since most owners do not disclose perks with them.

An owner of a business we sold consistently wrote business checks for his personal purchases and distributed them through various expense line items. Almost half of his $200,000 annual cash flow was documented in a general ledger with the individual check numbers, dates, amounts and descriptions of the perks. During the acquisitions process, this owner was able to substantiate 100% of his owner perks and received almost full price for his business. While we do not recommend this practice, a complete paper trail eliminates a sense of uncertainty when a buyer is in the due diligence stage.

Unreported cash

Many businesses take cash as a method of payment for services. There is a tendency on the part of some owners not to report a percentage of those cash receipts. There is a solution in this type of situation when proving cash flow. If it cannot be proven, it does not exist.

A good business broker will not get involved in cash hiding scenarios. If he represents the seller, at the appropriate time, the business broker will arrange for the buyer and seller to get together privately to talk about any issues of cash as a part of cash flow. For all intent and purposes unreported cash, while sexy to buyers, would add little to the established sale price. In fact, this will turn off many buyers.

Year-end

This area of bookkeeping is usually performed at the end of the year when the CPA calls to give the owner the news about his income tax exposure. Many owners play with costs to reduce their tax liability. Unfortunately, these owners are not concerned about the effect of their adjustments on the business performance related to cash flow; they are only concerned about lowering taxes. One of the main areas owners scrutinize is the ending inventory figure. They know that a lower ending inventory results in a higher cost of goods and a lower net profit, resulting in a lower income tax.

Another target area for many owners is the Cost of Goods section of the business's P&L. Everything, including owner's compensation, can end up in the cost of goods sold. The problem is, the resulting picture given to buyers is a very inconsistent gross profit, especially when evaluating several years of operation. Many times the owners themselves do not remember what they did and cannot explain it to buyers. This creates a nightmare for buyers going through due diligence, trying to understand the flow of the business. The business may be fine but a year-end adjustment can skew figures such as cost of goods and gross profit, creating a hazy picture that is difficult to explain.

Difficult People

Next to bad records, a seller or buyer with a difficult attitude is often the cause of a slow deal.

Very profitable businesses with great records, good cash flow and an outstanding history should have sold, but did not, due to an owner's personality and attitude. The selling process is a killer for everyone involved, especially the seller. The "I do not have to sell" or "Take it or leave it attitude" does not enhance the acquisition process. Selling a business must be treated like a marriage, not a divorce.

It is also important for the support team to display a good disposition. If a seller is happy with a deal, then move forward like you are going to a wedding.

Business brokers

An incompetent business broker can make life miserable or worse, kill a deal.

The potential signs of a business broker to avoid are: part-time brokers, real estate agents that attempt to do business brokerage on the side, new business brokers that are not part of a firm, part-time brokers who work out of their home, and management consultants. These types of brokers may close a few deals but as a seller, you are gambling on a mule in a horse race. Pick a voracious, aggressive broker who wants to win for you. You wouldn't hire a weak attorney to represent you in court, would you? You don't want to hire a weak or flunky real estate agent whose only focus is making a buck. You need the guy who is busy, who has plenty of buyers and who is ready to go to battle for you.

Support team
It takes an experienced team to successfully handle and complete business acquisitions. Attorneys, broker assistants, CPAs, business brokers, lenders, and others will need to work together to get a deal done.

If a seller has run a business for a number of years, he knows how difficult it is to ensure employees work together. Do not assume it could not be as difficult with your support team. The selling process is the time to use your management skills to ensure a seamless process.

Messy business
As discussed in the chapter on "Showing a Business", it is crucial to have an orderly and professional environment to show potential buyers. It is hard to change a buyer's first impression.

Continue the course of business
It's not over until the final documents are closed. Many business owners get so wrapped up in the process they do not pay the attention needed to run their business.
The acquisitions process is long and needs constant attention. Therefore, a deal could go on for months. If cash flow craters during that period, a buyer could back out of his contract. Sellers, who allow their cash flow trends and profitability to drop, if detected by a lender, are at risk of losing financing.

Incorrect information

Incorrect information can murder the process. Buyers remember everything and any inconsistency in the information provided could raise a red flag in their analysis.

15

I'm Not Ready Yet
Plan and Prepare for Selling Later

A competent business owner should always have an exit strategy when it comes to his business. Unless you are going to pass the business to a family member or eventually close the business, there will come a time when you will sell.

Increase cash flow
When the time comes, cash flow is equivalent to location in real estate. Cash flow is the main variable that buyers consistently review when they are evaluating a business. They are hesitant to purchase a business with cash flow on the decline. If they do, the value they are willing to pay is usually at a significant discount. Buyers are leery anyway since they feel that sellers must be hiding something. Decreasing cash flow is very difficult to validate as a reason for selling.

Get out of your own way
The business owner who reminds people of "Norm" from the sitcom "Cheers"-- where everybody knows your name--may be great for business but could be harmful when it selling the business.

In order to maximize the market value of a business, owners have to disassociate themselves from the business and have customers, employees, and suppliers sign on because of the business, not the owner.

The best method of removing yourself from a business is to train your right-hand person to take on some of your responsibilities, including dealing with customers, employees and suppliers.

Develop a management team

In addition to removing yourself as the point person, developing strong management is equally important. A buyer can review financials and inspect equipment and inventory to determine value. This analysis is clear-cut. One of the major factors that will move this value up or down is the quality of the employees. How long have they been there? Will there be key employees to assist the new owner with the business?

Replace family members

Having family member work in the business is one way to build a business. It could also be a huge detriment when the time comes to sell. A prospective buyer will be very concerned if a seller's wife, son, brother, etc., because he's skeptical of employee retention. Even if the family members agree to stay on after the business sells, the buyer might still have other doubts. It is common for family members to be paid more than a regular employee doing the same function. That could alarm a buyer. There might also be a perception that the family member may not be as qualified as he or she could be and got the position because of nepotism. This might lead a buyer to wonder if he is getting the best available person for the job.

Reduce the amount of untracked owner perks

Most small businesses owners "live" out of their business.

In the small business arena, if you have hired a good accountant, the net income on the year-end tax return is usually between $0 and $100,000. This does not mean the cash flow to the owner is low, since the difference is usually in salary and owner perks. These owner perks can include: health insurance, auto insurance, meals, entertainment, travel, and personal purchases. Even though these perks are valid, often first time buyers have a difficult time understanding them all and might dismiss them in their cash flow analysis.

EBITDA plus owner salary is the most common form of cash flow to a buyer. In a small business, owner perks can often be a large percentage of the total cash flow to owner. Since leading institutions and buyers focus on EBITDA, it would be wise to reduce or eliminate owner perks for one or two year prior to selling a business. In addition to reducing perks, it is mandatory that the perks you continue to expense be paid through specific and verifiable expense line items.

Sell off the unwanted inventory
When marketing a business, it is difficult to obtain a price based on the assessment of assets if they are not necessary for the operation of a business. By selling the assets in advance, the business owner gains added revenue from the sale of assets and a better business package to sell.. The sum of the parts should always be more than the whole when it comes to selling unnecessary assets and then the business. Get rid of the unnecessary items you have accumulated, tighten up.

Reduce inventory
Like unnecessary assets, inventory should be kept at a minimum in order to help keep costs low and help you set a selling price at a level to maximize the number of potential buyers.
A buyer will not pay for dead inventory. Before closing, most buyers will take inventory to ensure that what he is paying for is there and in good condition. Dead, obsolete and/or excess inventory can hinder a business sale. A buyer will only want the inventory that is necessary to run the business. If inventory levels are too high, the buyer might not be able to substantiate or afford the sale price with the excess inventory included.

Diversify the customers
The old adage, "Don't put all your eggs in one basket", applies to a business's customer base. Diversifying the customer base will not only increase the chances of selling a business, but also will help create a steady cash flow and reduce the impact of losing a customer.

Organization

Since key employees are vital to a business, an employee chart acts as an outstanding tool to summarize the team. The chart includes: tenure, pay, position, and description. Having a view of the staff will make it easier for a buyer to evaluate the employees and objectives.

Reduce unnecessary purchases

If large purchases are needed but not essential, let the buyer decide if he wants to make an investment. It will be easier to offer a business at a price that does not include a recent large purchase.

Additional steps used to prepare for a later sale

- Eliminate the fat when it comes to employees
- Have written procedures for operations (i.e. employee manuals)
- Have accounts receivables high
- Keep accounts payables low

Time to say goodbye?

For most people, selling a business is a whole lot easier than starting one, especially if you have professionals on your side who know how to show it in the best light and make the most of what you've built. The emotional turmoil of letting your baby go is often the hardest part. With experienced help by your side, you can avoid some of the emotional turmoil and many of the hassles that come with any complex and unique transaction. And every business is unique. Selling one is complex. Let Peterson Acquisitions help you prepare your exit strategy and assist you in selling when you are ready. We have a staff unmatched in the industry. We are here to help.

Call us at Peterson Acquisitions, 913-647-7500.